THE CANADIAN LIVING

COOKING
COLLECTION

ONE-DISH
MEALS

The following Canadian companies were involved in the production
of this Collection: Colour Technologies, Fred Bird & Associates Limited,
Gordon Sibley Design Inc., On-line Graphics, Telemedia Publishing Inc. and
The Madison Book Group Inc.

Canadian Living is a trademark of Telemedia Publishing Inc.
All trademark rights, registered and unregistered, are reserved.

We acknowledge the contribution of
Drew Warner, Joie Warner and Flavor Publications.

Produced by
The Madison Book Group Inc.
40 Madison Avenue
Toronto, Ontario
Canada
M5R 2S1

ONE-DISH MEALS

■ *On our cover:*
Provençal Beef Stew
(p. 10)

A meal in one dish — now that's a great idea! Here are rich, thick soups like *Haddock and Potato Chowder* and *Better-Next-Day Borscht* as well as slow-simmering stews like *Veal Paprika Stew with Carrots and Peppers* and *Easy Oyster Stew.* You'll also find comforting, old-fashioned favorites like *Beef Potpie, Lamb Casserole, Chicken and Biscuits* and *Layered Macaroni and Cheese Casserole.* Meatless can be marvelous with recipes like spicy *Vegetable Chili with Cheddar* and easy *Spaghetti Frittata.* We've even given you serving suggestions and tips so that, with the addition of a crisp salad and crusty bread, you can prepare a complete meal for a family supper or casual dinner with friends.

One-Dish Meals is just one of the eight full-color cookbooks that make up THE CANADIAN LIVING COOKING COLLECTION. Inside each of these colorful cookbooks are the kind of satisfying, easy-to-make dishes you'll want to cook over and over again. Each recipe in the Collection has been carefully selected and tested by *Canadian Living* to make sure it turns out wonderfully every time you make it. When you collect all eight cookbooks, you can choose from over 500 dishes — from marvelous soups to sensational desserts — all guaranteed to make any meal extra special.

Elizabeth Baird

Elizabeth Baird
Food Director, *Canadian Living* Magazine

Better-Next-Day Borscht

Like many thick soups, this beet and mixed vegetable borscht is better the day after it's made.

1-1/2 lb	beef bones	750 g
1 lb	chuck steak	500 g
15 cups	cold water	3.75 L
1-1/2 tsp	salt	7 mL
8	peppercorns	8
2 cups	diced peeled beets	500 mL
2 cups	cubed peeled potatoes	500 mL
1 cup	chopped carrots	250 mL
1 cup	chopped onion	250 mL
1/2 cup	sliced celery	125 mL
3 cups	shredded cabbage	750 mL
1	clove garlic, crushed	1
1-1/2 cups	chopped canned tomatoes	375 mL
2 tbsp	(approx) lemon juice	25 mL
	Salt and pepper	
1 cup	sour cream	250 mL
1/4 cup	chopped fresh dill	50 mL

■ In large stock pot, bring bones, steak, water, salt and peppercorns to boil, skimming off foam. Reduce heat and simmer, uncovered, until meat is tender, 1-1/2 to 2 hours. Remove and discard bones. Remove steak and cut into 1/2-inch (1 cm) cubes; set aside.

■ Strain stock through dampened cheesecloth into large saucepan. Add beets, potatoes, carrots, onion and celery; bring to boil. Reduce heat and simmer, covered, for 20 minutes. Add cabbage, garlic and tomatoes; simmer for 20 minutes or until all vegetables are tender.

■ Add meat and lemon juice, season with more lemon juice, salt and pepper to taste. Heat through. *(Soup can be prepared to this point, covered and refrigerated overnight; reheat before continuing.)* Ladle into soup bowls; top with dollop of sour cream and sprinkle with dill. Makes 8 to 10 servings.

(left) Better-Next-Day Borscht; (right) Haddock and Potato Chowder (p. 6) ▶

Haddock and Potato Chowder

If haddock is unavailable, substitute other firm white fish.

1 lb	haddock fillets	500 g
4 cups	water	1 L
1 tsp	salt	5 mL
3 cups	cubed peeled potatoes	750 mL
1 cup	chopped onion	250 mL
1 cup	chopped celery	250 mL
Pinch	pepper	Pinch
1 cup	milk, light cream or evaporated milk	250 mL
2 tbsp	butter	25 mL

■ In large saucepan, bring fish, water and salt to boil; reduce heat and simmer gently, uncovered, for 8 to 10 minutes or until opaque. With slotted spoon, remove fish and break into bite-size pieces; set aside.

■ Skim off any foam from fish stock. Add potatoes, onion, celery and pepper; cover and bring to boil. Reduce heat and simmer until tender.

■ Return fish to pan. Pour in milk and heat through without boiling. Taste and adjust seasoning. Swirl in butter. Makes 6 servings.

WONDERFUL CHOWDERS
Chowders are thick seafood soups that transform a bucket of clams or the catch of the day into supper for the whole family. They are quite simple — usually just fish, potato, onion and milk. You might like to add a few cooked shrimp, or a spoonful of fresh parsley or some crumbled bacon.

Autumn Soup with Sausage

This easy main-course soup can be made ahead, covered and refrigerated for up to 2 days, then reheated just before serving. Serve with corn bread and coleslaw. For dessert, spoon dollops of whipped cream over fresh peaches.

1 lb	sweet Italian sausages	500 g
2 tbsp	vegetable oil	25 mL
2	potatoes, peeled and diced	2
2	carrots, diced	2
2	stalks celery, diced	2
1	small rutabaga, diced	1
1	onion, chopped	1
Half	sweet green pepper, diced	Half
5 cups	beef stock	1.25 L
1/2 cup	dried red lentils, rinsed	125 mL
1 tbsp	tomato paste	15 mL
	Salt and pepper	
2 tbsp	chopped fresh parsley	25 mL

■ Cut sausages into 1-inch (2.5 cm) pieces. In large saucepan, heat 1 tbsp (15 mL) of the oil over medium heat; cook sausages for 3 minutes. Add potatoes; cook for about 2 minutes or until browned. Set aside in paper towel-lined dish.

■ Add remaining oil, carrots, celery, rutabaga, onion and green pepper to saucepan; cook for 3 to 5 minutes or just until vegetables are softened.

■ Stir in stock, lentils, tomato paste, and salt and pepper to taste. Bring to boil; reduce heat, cover and simmer for 20 minutes.

■ Add reserved sausages and potatoes; cover and simmer for 25 minutes or until vegetables are tender. Taste and adjust seasoning if necessary. Sprinkle with parsley. Makes 6 to 8 servings.

Lobster-Potato Chowder

Homey yet luxurious, nothing beats the taste of Maritime potatoes and lobster.
Make a meal out of this chowder with some crusty bread (or tea biscuits if you're in
the mood for baking) and a salad of the freshest greens available.

1	cooked lobster, cooled (about 1-1/4 lb/625 g)	1
1/4 cup	(approx) butter	50 mL
1-1/4 cups	finely chopped onions	300 mL
1/2 cup	chopped celery	125 mL
4 cups	cubed peeled potatoes	1 L
3/4 tsp	salt	4 mL
1/4 tsp	pepper	1 mL
2 cups	water	500 mL
2 cups	light cream	500 mL
1 cup	milk	250 mL
1/3 cup	finely chopped fresh parsley	75 mL

■ Crack lobster shell and remove meat. Cut into bite-size pieces and refrigerate until needed.

■ In large saucepan or stockpot, melt butter over medium heat; cook onions and celery, stirring often, for 5 minutes or until softened and translucent.

■ Stir in potatoes; season with salt and pepper. Add water; partially cover and bring to boil. Reduce heat and simmer until potatoes are tender, 15 to 20 minutes.

■ Pour in cream and milk; bring to simmer. Add lobster; cook until heated through. Taste and adjust seasoning if necessary. Pour into warmed soup tureen; sprinkle with parsley. Add dollop of butter if desired to streak chowder golden yellow. Makes 4 to 6 servings.

Tomato Chowder

Fish is best cooked just before serving, but you can make the chowder base when you have time to spare and freeze it for a later date or refrigerate it for up to 24 hours before serving if you wish. You can substitute any firm-fleshed fish such as cod or halibut. Crusty rolls and coleslaw with creamy dressing round out the meal.

1/4 cup	butter	50 mL
1 cup	coarsely chopped onions	250 mL
1 cup	sliced celery	250 mL
1/4 cup	chopped fresh parsley	50 mL
1	large clove garlic, chopped	1
1	can (28 oz/796 mL) tomatoes	1
1/2 cup	chicken stock	125 mL
1 tsp	dried basil	5 mL
1/2 tsp	coriander seeds, finely crushed	2 mL
1	bay leaf	1
3	carrots	3
1	small white turnip	1
1 lb	turbot fillets	500 g

■ In large saucepan, melt butter over medium heat; cook onions, celery, parsley and garlic, stirring, for 2 minutes. Cover and reduce heat to medium-low; cook for about 7 minutes or until onions are softened.

■ Stir in tomatoes, stock, basil, coriander seeds and bay leaf; simmer, covered and stirring occasionally, for 30 minutes.

■ Peel and coarsely dice carrots and turnip; add to chowder. Cook for 5 to 7 minutes or just until vegetables are tender-crisp. Remove bay leaf.

■ Meanwhile, cut fish into large chunks; add to chowder and cook for about 7 minutes or until fish is opaque and flakes easily when tested with fork. Makes about 6 servings.

SOUP OR STEW?

How to draw the line between soup and stew? It really is a question of thickness and the size of the ingredients. Usually, thicker and bigger is stew; thinner and smaller is soup — although what might be soup to some is stew to others. But that shouldn't matter as you pick up your spoon and savor a taste of a hearty dish made in the best tradition.

Provençal Beef Stew

Plenty of vegetables and a subtle orange twist update a beef stew. This delicious dish is pictured on our cover, too.

2 lb	blade roast, trimmed and cut in 1-inch (2.5 cm) cubes	1 kg
2 tbsp	all-purpose flour	25 mL
2 tbsp	olive oil	25 mL
4	cloves garlic, minced	4
1 tsp	dried thyme	5 mL
1	can (28 oz/796 mL) tomatoes (undrained)	1
1-1/2 cups	beef stock	375 mL
3 tbsp	red wine vinegar	50 mL
1/2 cup	orange juice	125 mL
2	bay leaves	2
	Rind of 1 orange, cut in strips	
1/4 tsp	pepper	1 mL
1/4 tsp	juniper berries (optional)	1 mL
4	large carrots, diagonally sliced	4
2 cups	small whole mushrooms	500 mL
2 cups	pearl onions, peeled (or cooking onions, quartered)	500 mL
1-1/2 cups	rotelle or other small pasta	375 mL
1/4 cup	chopped fresh parsley (optional)	50 mL
1/4 cup	pitted black olives	50 mL
	Fresh thyme sprigs	

■ Dredge meat lightly with flour. In large nonstick skillet, heat half of the oil over medium-high heat; cook meat, in batches and adding more oil as needed, for 6 to 8 minutes or until browned all over. Transfer to ovenproof casserole.

■ Drain oil from skillet; sauté garlic and thyme for 1 to 2 minutes or until garlic is softened. Pour in tomatoes, stock and vinegar, stirring to scrape up browned bits and mashing tomatoes with fork; bring to boil, then pour over meat.

■ To casserole, add orange juice, bay leaves, orange rind, pepper, and juniper berries (if using); cover and bake in 350°F (180°C) oven for 1 hour. Stir in carrots, mushrooms and onions; bake for 40 minutes.

■ Stir in pasta; bake for 20 minutes or until meat is tender. Let stand for 5 minutes. Remove bay leaves. Sprinkle with parsley (if using) and olives. Garnish with thyme sprigs. Makes 6 servings.

Polenta Lasagna

This hearty best-loved favorite has a new twist with cornmeal polenta layers instead of noodles. If you hesitate at the word polenta, take courage. It's surprisingly easy to make, colorful and delicious.

6 cups	water	1.5 L
1/2 tsp	salt	2 mL
1-1/2 cups	cornmeal	375 mL
2 tsp	olive oil	10 mL
1 lb	lean ground beef	500 g
2 cups	chopped onions	500 mL
5	cloves garlic, minced	5
1-1/2 cups	sliced mushrooms	375 mL
1	sweet red or green pepper, diced	1
1	can (19 oz/540 mL) tomatoes	1
1	can (14 oz/398 mL) tomato sauce	1
1/2 tsp	hot pepper flakes	2 mL
1/4 cup	minced fresh parsley	50 mL
	Salt and pepper	
1	pkg (10 oz/284 g) fresh spinach, trimmed	1
2 cups	shredded mozzarella cheese	500 mL

■ In large saucepan, bring water and salt to boil over high heat; gradually pour in cornmeal, stirring constantly. Reduce heat and simmer, stirring frequently, for 10 to 15 minutes or until smooth and thickened enough to mound on spoon.

■ Transfer to greased 13- × 9-inch (3 L) baking dish; smooth top and set aside to set. *(Recipe can be prepared to this point and refrigerated, covered, for up to 2 days.)*

■ Meanwhile, in large heavy saucepan or Dutch oven, heat half of the oil over high heat; cook beef, stirring, for 5 minutes or until no longer pink. Remove and set aside.

■ Drain off fat in pan. Reduce heat to medium and add remaining oil; cook onions, garlic, mushrooms and red pepper until softened, about 5 minutes.

■ Add tomatoes, crushing lightly with fork. Stir in tomato sauce, meat and hot pepper flakes; bring to boil. Reduce heat and simmer, uncovered, until thickened, about 55 minutes. Add parsley; season with salt and pepper to taste. *(Sauce can be cooled, covered and refrigerated for up to 2 days, or frozen for up to 2 months. Thaw before continuing.)*

■ Meanwhile, rinse spinach; shake off excess water. With just the water clinging to leaves, cook spinach for 4 minutes. Drain and squeeze out as much moisture as possible; chop and set aside.

■ Turn polenta out onto chopping board; with long knife, cut horizontally into 2 layers. (Don't worry if polenta breaks.) Spread about 1 cup (250 mL) of the sauce in same baking dish; cover with 1 layer of the polenta. Add half of the spinach, sauce and cheese. Repeat with remaining polenta, spinach, sauce and cheese. *(Recipe can be prepared to this point, cooled, covered and refrigerated for up to 2 days or frozen for up to 2 months. Thaw before continuing.)*

■ Bake in 375°F (190°C) oven for about 50 minutes or until crusty and bubbling. Makes 8 to 10 servings.

Beef Potpie

For extra flavor, use 1/2 lb (250 g) beef kidney and 1 lb (500 g) beef instead of all beef.

1/4 cup	all-purpose flour	50 mL
1 tsp	salt	5 mL
1/4 tsp	pepper	1 mL
1-1/2 lb	boneless beef (stewing or round), cut into 1-inch (2.5 cm) cubes	750 g
1/4 cup	vegetable oil	50 mL
2	large onions, chopped	2
2	cloves garlic, minced	2
1/2 cup	chopped celery	125 mL
1/2 lb	mushrooms, thickly sliced	250 g
2 cups	hot beef stock	500 mL
1	bay leaf	1
1 tsp	dried thyme	5 mL
1/2 tsp	dried basil	2 mL
2 cups	cooked cubed peeled potatoes	500 mL
1-1/2 cups	sliced cooked carrots	375 mL
1/4 cup	chopped fresh parsley	50 mL
	Pastry for single-crust pie (or 4 oz/125 g frozen puff pastry)	

■ Combine flour, salt and pepper; dredge meat in mixture.

■ In large skillet, heat oil over medium-high heat; cook meat until well browned all over. Add onions, garlic and celery; cook for 3 to 4 minutes or until softened. Add mushrooms; cook for 3 minutes, stirring often.

■ Stir in any remaining flour; add stock and cook, stirring, until thickened and boiling. Add bay leaf, thyme and basil; cover and simmer over low heat for 1-1/2 hours or until beef is tender. Discard bay leaf. Stir in potatoes, carrots and parsley; transfer to 10-cup (2.5 L) baking dish. Taste and adjust seasoning.

■ On lightly floured surface, roll out pastry and fit over beef mixture, sealing to edge of dish.

■ Cut slits for steam vents. Bake in 400°F (200°C) oven for 25 minutes or until pastry is golden and mixture is hot. Makes 6 servings.

(centre) Beef Potpie ▶

Pork Ragout with Sweet Potatoes

Use well-trimmed pork butt for this tasty ragout. Complete the meal with a refreshing lemon mousse.

1/3 cup	packed brown sugar	75 mL
1/3 cup	all-purpose flour	75 mL
3 lb	pork butt, cut in 1-inch (2.5 cm) cubes	1.5 kg
1/4 cup	Dijon mustard	50 mL
3 tbsp	vegetable oil	50 mL
1	onion, chopped	1
2	cloves garlic, minced	2
1-1/3 cups	chicken stock	325 mL
1 cup	dry sherry	250 mL
6	sweet potatoes (about 3 lb/1.5 kg)	6
1/2 tsp	salt	2 mL
1/2 tsp	pepper	2 mL
1/4 cup	chopped fresh parsley	50 mL

■ In shallow dish, combine sugar with flour. Coat pork cubes lightly in mustard; dredge in sugar mixture.

■ In large nonstick skillet, heat oil over medium heat; cook pork, a layer at a time, until browned on all sides. With slotted spoon, transfer to large Dutch oven. Add onion and garlic to skillet; cook until softened, about 3 minutes. Remove with slotted spoon to Dutch oven.

■ Discard any fat in skillet; pour in chicken stock and sherry. Bring to boil and cook for 1 minute, stirring to scrape up browned bits from bottom of pan. Add to Dutch oven.

■ Peel sweet potatoes; cut into 1-inch (2.5 cm) cubes. In large saucepan of boiling water, cook potatoes until barely tender, about 3 minutes. Drain and add to Dutch oven.

■ Cover and bake in 350°F (180°C) oven until meat is tender, about 45 minutes. Add salt and pepper. *(Ragout can be cooled, covered and refrigerated overnight. Reheat, uncovered, in 375°F/190°C oven until heated through, 30 to 40 minutes.)* Sprinkle with parsley. Makes about 8 servings.

Hunter's Pie

This more highly flavored version of old-fashioned shepherd's pie is wonderful served with a beet and onion salad. The pie can be frozen, but omit the potato topping. Cook and spread the potatoes on the thawed casserole just before baking.

2 tbsp	butter	25 mL
1 tbsp	vegetable oil	15 mL
1/2 cup	chopped onion	125 mL
1/2 cup	chopped celery	125 mL
1/4 cup	chopped fresh parsley	50 mL
1	clove garlic, minced	1
1	large carrot, grated or finely chopped	1
1 lb	lean ground beef	500 g
1/2 lb	ground veal	250 g
1/2 cup	beef stock	125 mL
1 tbsp	horseradish	15 mL
1 tsp	dry mustard	5 mL
1/2 tsp	salt	2 mL
1/4 tsp	each ginger, dried thyme and black pepper	1 mL
Pinch	each cinnamon and allspice (optional)	Pinch
2 lb	potatoes (about 7), peeled and halved	1 kg
1/2 cup	milk	125 mL
	White pepper	
1	egg, beaten	1

■ In large skillet, heat 1 tbsp (15 mL) of the butter with oil over medium heat; cook onion, celery, parsley, garlic and carrot, stirring, for 2 minutes. Reduce heat to medium-low; cook for 7 minutes longer or until onions are softened. Transfer to 9-inch (2.5 L) square baking dish; set aside.

■ Add beef and veal to skillet and increase heat to medium-high; cook until evenly browned, breaking up large pieces. Add to onion mixture.

■ Pour stock into skillet; bring to simmer, stirring to scrape up any browned bits from bottom of pan. Remove from heat; stir in horseradish, mustard, salt, ginger, thyme, black pepper, and cinnamon and allspice (if using). Add to meat mixture and combine thoroughly.

■ In saucepan of lightly salted boiling water, cook potatoes until tender; drain well. Remove 3 halves and set aside to cool. Mash potatoes with milk, remaining 1 tbsp (15 mL) butter, and white pepper to taste until fluffy; set aside.

■ Slice reserved potatoes; layer over meat mixture. Spread mashed potatoes evenly on top; score with fork. *(Recipe can be prepared to this point, covered and refrigerated for up to 48 hours.)* Brush egg over topping; bake in 425°F (220°C) oven for 15 minutes. Reduce heat to 350°F (180°C) and bake for 30 minutes longer. Makes about 6 servings.

Ragout de Boulettes

"Meatball stew" doesn't convey the spicy goodness of these lean pork meatballs simmered in broth. They are perfectly delicious with a sprinkle of parsley and a bowl of fluffy mashed potatoes or buttered noodles.

2	slices white bread	2
1/2 cup	milk	125 mL
2 tbsp	butter	25 mL
3/4 cup	minced onion	175 mL
2 lb	ground lean pork	1 kg
3 tbsp	minced fresh parsley	50 mL
2 tsp	salt	10 mL
1 tsp	dry mustard	5 mL
1/2 tsp	cinnamon	2 mL
1/2 tsp	pepper	2 mL
1/4 tsp	each cloves, ginger and nutmeg	1 mL
4 cups	beef or chicken stock	1 L
1/2 cup	all-purpose flour	125 mL
3/4 cup	cold water	175 mL
	Finely chopped fresh parsley (optional)	

■ Crumb or cube bread very finely; soak in milk for 5 minutes.

■ In large skillet, melt 1 tbsp (15 mL) of the butter; cook onion until tender. Transfer to large bowl; add pork, bread mixture, parsley, salt, mustard, cinnamon, pepper, cloves, ginger and nutmeg. Mix thoroughly; form into 2-inch (5 cm) balls.

■ In skillet, melt remaining butter over medium heat; brown meatballs, one layer at a time, on all sides. Place in saucepan; set aside.

■ Pour off fat. Pour 1 cup (250 mL) of the stock into skillet; heat, scraping up browned bits from bottom of pan. Pour over meatballs; pour in remaining stock. Simmer, partially covered, for 1-1/4 hours. Taste and adjust seasoning.

■ In clean skillet, cook flour over medium heat, stirring frequently, until golden. In jar with tight-fitting lid, shake flour with cold water until smooth; gradually pour into simmering stew, stirring constantly, and cook until thickened. Simmer for 10 minutes.

■ Sprinkle generously with parsley (if using). Makes 6 to 8 servings.

Cajun-Style Chili with Pork

Cajun cooking, developed by the descendants of the Acadians who fled to Louisiana more than 200 years ago, is based on local ingredients such as hot and sweet peppers, onions, celery, pork and seafood. If you prefer a more traditional chili flavor, use cumin instead of oregano, and add chili powder to taste.

2 lb	ground pork	1 kg
2	large onions, chopped	2
4	cloves garlic, minced	4
1	each sweet red and green pepper, chopped	1
3	stalks celery, chopped	3
1	can (28 oz/796 mL) tomatoes	1
1	can (28 oz/796 mL) kidney beans, drained	1
1/4 tsp	hot pepper flakes	1 mL
1 tsp	dried oregano	5 mL
1/4 tsp	cayenne pepper	1 mL
Dash	hot pepper sauce	Dash
	Salt and pepper	

■ In large Dutch oven or heavy saucepan, cook pork over medium heat, stirring to break up meat, for about 5 minutes or until browned. Pour off fat.

■ Add onions; cook until tender. Add garlic, red and green peppers and celery; cook, stirring occasionally, for 5 minutes or until vegetables are softened.

■ Add tomatoes, breaking up with back of spoon. Stir in kidney beans, hot pepper flakes, oregano, cayenne pepper, hot pepper sauce, and salt and pepper to taste. Bring to boil; reduce heat and simmer for 20 minutes.

■ *(Casserole can be cooled, covered and refrigerated for up to 2 days or frozen for up to 3 months. Thaw before reheating in 350°F/180°C oven for 40 to 50 minutes or over medium heat, uncovered and stirring occasionally, for 20 minutes.)* Makes about 8 servings.

Main-Course Potato Salad

Chopped cucumber can be substituted for the dill pickles, if desired, in this quick, satisfying salad, which you can serve warm or cold.

6	red potatoes (unpeeled)	6
2 cups	julienned cooked pork loin	500 mL
1/2 cup	chopped green onions	125 mL
1/4 cup	chopped dill pickles	50 mL
2	hard-cooked eggs, chopped	2
1	bunch watercress (optional)	1
	DRESSING	
1/2 cup	olive oil	125 mL
2 tbsp	minced fresh parsley	25 mL
2 tbsp	cider vinegar or white wine vinegar	25 mL

1	clove garlic, minced	1
1 tsp	Dijon mustard	5 mL
1/2 tsp	salt	2 mL
1/4 tsp	pepper	1 mL

■ In saucepan of lightly salted boiling water, cook potatoes just until tender, 15 to 20 minutes. Drain and shake over low heat for a few minutes to dry. Cut into bite-size chunks or quarters. Arrange in bowl. Top with rows of pork, onions, pickles and eggs.

■ **Dressing:** Whisk together oil, parsley, vinegar, garlic, mustard, salt and pepper; drizzle over warm salad. *(Salad can be covered and refrigerated for up to 4 hours to serve cold.)* Garnish with watercress (if using) just before serving. Makes 4 servings.

Braised Italian-Style Beef

A low-cost alternative to the usual Sunday roast, this savory beef dish is easy to prepare and might give you enough leftovers for another meal.

3 lb	boneless cross rib or blade roast	1.5 kg
2	cloves garlic, slivered	2
1/4 tsp	each salt and pepper	1 mL
1 tbsp	all-purpose flour	15 mL
2 tbsp	vegetable oil	25 mL
2	onions, coarsely chopped	2
3	carrots, coarsely chopped	3
1	stalk celery, chopped	1
1 tsp	dried thyme	5 mL
1	bay leaf	1
1 cup	beef stock, tomato juice or dry red wine	250 mL
1 cup	chopped drained canned tomatoes	250 mL
1 tbsp	chopped fresh parsley	15 mL
1 tsp	each dried oregano and basil	5 mL

■ With sharp knife, make small cuts in beef; insert garlic sliver in each. Rub meat with salt and pepper; sprinkle with flour.

■ In deep heavy saucepan or Dutch oven, heat oil over high heat; sear meat for about 7 minutes or until browned all over.

■ Add onions, carrots, celery, thyme, bay leaf and stock. Cover tightly and simmer over low heat for 1-1/2 hours, turning beef occasionally.

■ Stir in tomatoes, parsley, oregano and basil; simmer for 45 to 50 minutes or until beef is tender. Discard bay leaf. Slice and serve with vegetables and sauce. Makes 6 servings.

BRAISING
Braising combines the quick cooking of browning with slow, flavorful simmering. It's a method that can be used with delicious results for fish, chicken, meat and vegetables.

• To start, brown ingredients in hot fat or oil over high heat to seal in the juices and add flavor. Next, place all meat and/or vegetables in a heavy pan and add enough liquid to moisten, not cover. The dish then simmers until tender.

Creamy Ham Scallop

This hearty dish is sure to please adults and kids alike. It makes a great Boxing Day lunch or supper and can be frozen for up to six weeks.

2 lb	cooked ham	1 kg
1	small cauliflower	1
4	carrots, sliced	4
4	stalks celery, sliced	4
2 tbsp	butter	25 mL
1 tbsp	vegetable oil	15 mL
2	onions, chopped	2
2	cloves garlic, minced	2
1/4 cup	all-purpose flour	50 mL
1/2 tsp	dry mustard	2 mL
1/2 tsp	pepper	2 mL
2 cups	chicken stock	500 mL
1 cup	milk	250 mL
	TOPPING	
1 cup	whole wheat cracker crumbs	250 mL
1 cup	shredded Edam cheese	250 mL
1/2 cup	sliced almonds	125 mL
1/4 cup	freshly grated Parmesan cheese	50 mL

■ Cut ham into bite-size cubes. Separate cauliflower into bite-size florets. In large pot of boiling salted water, cook cauliflower, carrots and celery for 7 minutes or until tender-crisp. Drain and set aside.

■ In same pot, melt butter with oil over medium heat; cook onions and garlic for 4 minutes or until onions are softened. Stir in flour, mustard and pepper; cook, stirring, for 1 minute.

■ Gradually stir in chicken stock; bring to boil. Reduce heat and simmer for 2 minutes or until thickened, stirring frequently. Stir in milk; add ham, cauliflower, carrots and celery. Spoon into shallow 10-cup (2.5 L) casserole.

■ **Topping:** Combine cracker crumbs, Edam, almonds and Parmesan; sprinkle over casserole. *(Recipe can be prepared to this point, covered and refrigerated for up 2 days or frozen for up to 6 weeks. To reheat, thaw first.)* Bake, uncovered, in 375°F (190°C) oven for 30 to 40 minutes or until heated through and top is golden brown. Makes 6 to 8 servings.

Meat Loaf with Peppercorn Mushroom Sauce

Meat loaf with panache, chock-full of vegetables and drenched with an elegant wild mushroom sauce, is worthy of any Sunday dinner.

1	egg	1
1 cup	fresh bread crumbs	250 mL
1	small onion, minced	1
Half	each small carrot and celery stalk, finely chopped	Half
1	clove garlic, minced	1
1/3 cup	finely chopped mushrooms	75 mL
3 tbsp	minced fresh parsley	50 mL
1 tsp	dried tarragon	5 mL
1/2 tsp	salt	2 mL
1/2 tsp	dried thyme	2 mL
1/4 tsp	pepper	1 mL
Pinch	each nutmeg and cloves	Pinch
1-3/4 lb	lean ground beef	875 g

MUSHROOM SAUCE

1/2 oz	dried porcini mushrooms	15 g
1/2 cup	warm water	125 mL
1/4 cup	butter	50 mL
1	clove garlic, minced	1
1	each small onion and carrot, diced	1
1 cup	sliced fresh mushrooms	250 mL
1 tbsp	all-purpose flour	15 mL
1 cup	beef stock	250 mL
1/4 cup	dry red wine	50 mL
1 tsp	tomato paste	5 mL
2 tbsp	light cream	25 mL
1 tsp	crushed peppercorns	5 mL

■ In bowl, mix egg, bread crumbs, onion, carrot, celery, garlic, mushrooms, parsley, tarragon, salt, thyme, pepper, nutmeg and cloves; mix in meat. Press into 9- × 5-inch (2 L) loaf pan; bake in 350°F (180°C) oven about 1 hour or until meat thermometer registers 170°F (75°C). Drain off pan drippings and discard.

■ **Mushroom Sauce:** Meanwhile, soak dried mushrooms in warm water for about 30 minutes or until softened. Drain, reserving soaking liquid; chop mushrooms finely.

■ In skillet, melt butter over medium heat; cook rehydrated mushrooms, garlic, onion, carrot and fresh mushrooms until softened, 3 to 5 minutes. Sprinkle with flour, stirring. Blend in stock, wine and tomato paste. Strain reserved mushroom soaking liquid through cheesecloth and add to pan. Bring to boil; reduce heat and simmer until vegetables are softened and sauce has reduced enough to coat spoon, about 5 minutes. Stir in cream and peppercorns; taste and adjust seasoning.

■ Transfer meat loaf to warm serving platter and serve with sauce. Makes about 6 servings.

Round-Steak Fajitas

From the American southwest come fajitas *(pronounced fa-hee-tas), a chili-flavored stir-fry served in tortillas.*

2	wheat tortillas, (12 inches/30 cm)	2
Half	avocado, peeled and sliced	Half
1	tomato, chopped	1
1/4 cup	chopped fresh coriander or parsley	50 mL
2	lime wedges	2
1/4 cup	sour cream	50 mL
	FAJITAS	
6 oz	inside round steak	175 g
3/4 cup	sweet green pepper strips	175 mL
1	small onion, cut in strips	1
1 tbsp	Worcestershire sauce	15 mL
1 tbsp	vegetable oil	15 mL
1 tbsp	lime or lemon juice	15 mL
1	clove garlic, slivered	1
1/2 tsp	cumin	2 mL
1/4 tsp	paprika	1 mL
Dash	hot pepper sauce	Dash
	Salt	

■ **Fajitas:** Cut steak across the grain into strips 1-1/2 inches (4 cm) long and 1/8 inch (3 mm) thick. In bowl, combine steak, green pepper, onion, Worcestershire sauce, 1 tsp (5 mL) of the oil, lime juice, garlic,

cumin, paprika and hot pepper sauce. Marinate for 20 minutes at room temperature or for up to 12 hours in refrigerator. Drain, reserving marinade.

■ In large skillet, heat remaining oil over high heat. Add drained meat mixture; cook, stir-ring, until vegetables are softened and meat is tender, 3 to 4 minutes. Add reserved marinade; cook for about 1 minute to glaze meat. Season with salt to taste.

■ Meanwhile, warm tortillas in oven. Spoon meat mixture along middle of tortillas. Garnish with avocado, tomato, coriander and lime; spoon sour cream over. Fold up bottom of tortilla over filling; fold in sides. Makes 2 servings.

Skillet Pork with Harvest Vegetables

In this easy one-pan meal, pork is braised with potatoes, then beans and squash are layered on top. For a quick dessert, sauté apple slices.

1-1/2 lb	lean pork shoulder	750 g
1 tbsp	vegetable oil	15 mL
8	small red potatoes, halved	8
2 tsp	finely chopped fresh sage (or 1/2 tsp/2 mL dried)	10 mL
	Salt and pepper	
1/2 cup	chicken stock or water	125 mL
1-1/2 lb	butternut or hubbard squash	750 g
1/2 lb	green beans, trimmed	250 g

■ Slice pork thinly across the grain. In large skillet or Dutch oven, heat oil over medium-high heat; brown pork.

■ Add potatoes to skillet; sprinkle with sage, and salt and pepper to taste. Stir in stock; bring to boil. Reduce heat, cover and simmer for 20 minutes.

■ Meanwhile, peel, seed and cut squash into 2-inch (5 cm) chunks. Layer squash and green beans over potatoes and pork; bring to boil. Reduce heat, cover and simmer for about 20 minutes or until pork and vegetables are tender. Makes about 4 servings.

Sloppy Joes in Pita Bread

Light spicy Mexican-style pitas make a filling and satisfying meal. Sprinkle a variety of toppings over the meat, such as chopped tomatoes, shredded lettuce, chopped red or green peppers and celery, shredded Cheddar or partly skimmed mozzarella cheese.

6 oz	lean ground beef	175 g
1/4 cup	finely chopped onion	50 mL
1	small clove garlic, chopped	1
1/4 cup	chopped sweet green pepper	50 mL
1/2 tsp	chili powder	2 mL
1/4 tsp	cumin	1 mL
1/4 tsp	salt	1 mL
1/2 cup	tomato juice	125 mL
2	whole wheat pita breads (about 6 inches/15 cm)	2

■ In skillet, brown beef lightly over medium-high heat, breaking up with fork, for 5 to 7 minutes or until no longer pink.

■ Add onion, garlic and green pepper; cook until tender. Drain off any fat. Add chili powder, cumin and salt; stir in tomato juice and simmer for 3 minutes.

■ Warm pita breads; halve and fill with meat mixture. Makes 2 servings.

Lamb Casserole

Good crusty bread or rolls are all you need to serve with this casserole for a hearty winter supper. This freezes well, too.

2 lb	boneless lamb shoulder	1 kg
1 tbsp	lemon juice	15 mL
	Salt and pepper	
4	carrots	4
2	parsnips	2
2	small white turnips	2
3 tbsp	vegetable oil	50 mL
1/4 cup	chopped fresh parsley	50 mL
1	large clove garlic	1
2-1/2 cups	chicken stock	625 mL
1	can (5-1/2 oz/156 mL) tomato paste	1
1/2 cup	water	125 mL
1 tsp	granulated sugar	5 mL
1/2 tsp	dried basil	2 mL
10	small white cooking onions (walnut-size)	10

■ Trim visible fat from lamb; cut meat into 1-1/2-inch (4 cm) cubes. In shallow dish, sprinkle lamb with lemon juice; season with salt and pepper to taste. Toss to combine well; let stand for 30 minutes. Peel and cut carrots, parsnips and turnips into walnut-size chunks; set aside.

■ In large heavy saucepan, heat 1 tbsp (15 mL) of the oil over medium-low heat; cook parsley and garlic for about 5 minutes or until garlic has softened. Remove to plate; set aside.

■ Pour remaining oil into pan and increase heat to medium-high; brown meat in batches and remove to plate with parsley mixture.

■ Stir stock, tomato paste, water, sugar and basil into pan; bring to simmer, stirring to scrape up any browned bits from bottom of pan. Return meat and parsley mixture to pan; simmer, covered, for 40 to 45 minutes or until lamb is tender.

■ Add onions, carrots, parsnips and turnips; simmer for about 15 minutes or until vegetables are cooked. Season with salt and pepper to taste. Makes about 6 servings.

Veal Paprika Stew with Carrots and Green Peppers

If you're freezing this stew, make up to the point just before adding mushrooms and peppers; the freshly cooked peppers will have crisper texture.

4 lb	trimmed lean stewing veal, cut in 1-inch (2.5 cm) cubes	2 kg
1/4 cup	all-purpose flour	50 mL
1/3 cup	(approx) vegetable oil	75 mL
4	large onions, chopped	4
2 tbsp	sweet Hungarian paprika	25 mL
1-1/2 tsp	salt	7 mL
1 tsp	pepper	5 mL
1/2 tsp	caraway seeds	2 mL
2 cups	dry white wine	500 mL
2 cups	chicken stock	500 mL
1/4 cup	tomato paste	50 mL
1 lb	mini carrots	500 g
3 tbsp	butter	50 mL
4 cups	small mushrooms	1 L
2	sweet green or red peppers, diced	2

■ Dust veal lightly with flour. In large heavy saucepan, heat 2 tbsp (25 mL) of the oil over high heat; brown veal, in batches, adding up to 2 tbsp (25 mL) more oil if needed. Remove veal; set aside.

■ Add remaining oil to pan; cook onions over medium heat until softened, about 5 minutes. Return veal to pan; stir in paprika, salt, pepper and caraway seeds. Cook, stirring, for 3 minutes.

■ Add wine, stock and tomato paste; bring to boil. Reduce heat and simmer, covered, for 1 hour. Add carrots; cook for 15 minutes longer.

■ In large skillet, melt butter over medium heat; cook mushrooms and green peppers until slightly tender, about 4 minutes. Add to veal mixture; cook for about 15 minutes longer or until veal is fork-tender and carrots are tender. Remove from heat. Using slotted spoon, remove veal and vegetables; set aside.

■ Return saucepan to high heat and boil liquid, stirring, for about 5 minutes or until thick enough to coat spoon. Return veal and vegetables to liquid; heat through. Taste and adjust seasoning. Makes 12 servings.

Devilled Chicken Livers

Easy-on-the-budget chicken livers in a lively, colorful sauce make a warming main dish on chilly winter days. Accompany with rice or pasta and a salad.

1 lb	chicken livers	500 g
1/4 cup	all-purpose flour	50 mL
2 tsp	chili powder	10 mL
	Salt and pepper	
1 tbsp	butter	15 mL
2 tbsp	vegetable oil	25 mL
1	small sweet green pepper, cut in rings	1
1 cup	thinly sliced onions	250 mL
1 tsp	chopped seeded jalapeño pepper	5 mL
1	clove garlic, minced	1
1	can (19 oz/540 mL) tomatoes	1
1/2 cup	chicken stock	125 mL
Dash	hot pepper sauce	Dash

■ Trim and halve chicken livers. Combine flour, chili powder, and salt and pepper to taste. In bag, combine half of the livers with half of the flour mixture; shake to coat well and set aside. Repeat with remaining livers and flour mixture.

■ In skillet, heat butter with 1 tbsp (15 mL) of the oil over medium heat; cook green pepper, onions, jalapeño pepper and garlic until onions are softened. Transfer to casserole dish.

■ Add remaining oil to skillet and increase heat to medium-high; cook livers, in batches, just until firm and still pink inside, 4 to 5 minutes. Add to onion mixture.

■ Add tomatoes to skillet, breaking up with fork. Pour in stock and cook for 5 minutes, stirring to scrape up any browned bits from bottom of pan. Reduce heat to medium; simmer until sauce has thickened and is reduced by about one-third. Stir in hot pepper sauce, and salt and pepper to taste.

■ Spoon sauce over liver mixture and stir gently to combine. *(Recipe can be prepared to this point, cooled, covered and frozen; transfer to refrigerator night before serving.)* Bake, covered, in 325°F (160°C) oven for 45 to 50 minutes or until heated through. Makes about 4 servings.

Chicken and Biscuits

This dish can be mostly made in advance and kept refrigerated for a day. Then just make the biscuits and bake with the stew. (If using a stewing hen, increase simmering time to 4 hours to tenderize bird.)

STOCK

1	chicken (5 lb/2.5 kg)	1
5 cups	cold water	1.25 L
1	each onion, leek, carrot and celery stalk (with leaves), coarsely chopped	1
1 tbsp	salt	15 mL
5	each peppercorns and parsley stalks	5
1 tsp	crushed dried thyme	5 mL
2	bay leaves	2

STEW

12	small onions	12
6	carrots	6
1/4 lb	button mushrooms	125 g
1 cup	frozen peas	250 mL
1/3 cup	butter	75 mL
1/2 cup	all-purpose flour	125 mL
1 cup	light cream or milk	250 mL
1/4 cup	chopped fresh parsley	50 mL
1 tbsp	Worcestershire sauce	15 mL
1/4 tsp	each nutmeg and pepper	1 mL
Dash	hot pepper sauce	Dash

BISCUITS

2 cups	all-purpose flour	500 mL
4 tsp	baking powder	20 mL
1 tsp	salt	5 mL
1/2 cup	shortening	125 mL
1 cup	milk	250 mL

■ **Stock:** In large pot, bring chicken and water to boil; reduce heat and simmer for 15 minutes. Skim off foam. Add onion, leek, carrot, celery, salt, peppercorns, parsley, thyme and bay leaves; simmer gently, partially covered, for about 2 hours or until chicken is tender and no longer pink inside and meat almost falls off bones.

■ Remove chicken and let cool enough to handle; discard skin and bones. Chop meat into bite-size cubes; set aside. Strain stock into large saucepan, discarding vegetables.

■ **Stew:** Cut shallow "X" in root end of each onion. Chop carrots into 1-1/2-inch (4 cm) chunks. Add onions and carrots to stock; cover and simmer until tender. Using slotted spoon, remove vegetables and add to chicken.

■ Add mushrooms to stock; simmer for 4 minutes. Add peas; simmer for 1 minute. Remove and add to chicken and vegetables.

■ In separate saucepan, melt butter; stir in flour and cook over medium heat for 3 minutes without browning. Whisk in 3-1/4 cups (800 mL) of the hot stock; cook, stirring, until thickened. Add cream, parsley, Worcestershire sauce, nutmeg, pepper and hot pepper sauce; taste and adjust seasoning, adding more stock to thin if desired. Pour into large Dutch oven or casserole; add reserved chicken and vegetables and stir to mix.

■ **Biscuits:** In large bowl, combine flour, baking powder and salt; cut in shortening to make crumbly mixture. Stir in milk; form dough into ball. On lightly floured surface, roll out to 3/4-inch (2 cm) thickness; cut out rounds and place on top of stew. Bake, uncovered, in 425°F (220°C) oven for 20 to 25 minutes or until bubbling and biscuits are golden. Makes 6 to 8 servings.

Chicken Potpie

Use some leftover ham to make this delicious pie to tuck away in the freezer. Make sure the onions are about 1-1/2 inches (4 cm) in diameter. A salad of spinach, bean sprouts and mushrooms adds pleasing texture and color contrast.

2	large chicken breasts (about 1-1/2 lb/750 g)	2
1-1/2 cups	chicken stock	375 mL
3	sprigs parsley	3
2	sprigs celery leaf	2
1	bay leaf	1
2	carrots	2
8	small cooking onions	8
1 cup	cubed ham	250 mL
1 cup	frozen peas	250 mL
2 tbsp	all-purpose flour	25 mL
2 tbsp	butter, softened	25 mL
	Salt and pepper	
	Pastry for 8-inch (20 cm) single-crust pie	
	Milk	

■ In deep skillet, bring chicken, stock, parsley, celery and bay leaves to simmer; cover and cook over medium-low heat for 20 minutes.

■ Cut carrots into 1-inch (2.5 cm) pieces; add to skillet along with onions; cook for about 10 minutes or just until vegetables are cooked but still firm.

■ With slotted spoon, remove chicken and let cool; transfer carrots and onions to 6-cup (1.5 L) casserole. Discard parsley, celery and bay leaves. Discard skin and bones from chicken; cut meat into 1-1/2-inch (4 cm) chunks and add to casserole along with ham and peas.

■ In small dish, blend flour with butter until smooth; stir in a few tablespoonfuls (15 mL) of the stock to make thin paste. Blend back into remaining stock in skillet; bring to simmer and cook, stirring constantly, until thickened and bubbly, 3 to 4 minutes. Simmer gently for 5 minutes longer; do not let boil. Season with salt and pepper to taste. Pour into casserole and refrigerate while preparing pastry.

■ On lightly floured surface, roll out pastry and fit over cooled mixture in casserole; turn under edges and crimp. *(Recipe can be prepared to this point, covered and frozen. Transfer to refrigerator night before serving.)*

■ Brush lightly with milk; cut 1-inch (2.5 cm) circle in centre for steam vent. Bake in 425°F (220°C) oven for 10 minutes; reduce heat to 350°F (180°C) and bake for 50 to 60 minutes longer or until filling is bubbly. If pastry darkens too quickly, cover lightly with foil. Makes about 4 servings.

Turkey and Wild Rice Casserole

Use leftovers from the big bird to make this tasty casserole.

1 cup	wild rice	250 mL
3 cups	boiling water	750 mL
2 tbsp	butter	25 mL
1	small onion, chopped	1
1-1/2 cups	sliced mushrooms	375 mL
3 cups	diced cooked turkey	750 mL
1/2 cup	turkey or chicken stock	125 mL
1 cup	whipping cream	250 mL
1	can (10 oz/284 mL) water chestnuts, drained and sliced	1
1/4 cup	diced pimiento	50 mL
1 tsp	salt	5 mL
	Pepper	
1 cup	shredded Cheddar cheese	250 mL

■ In strainer, rinse rice thoroughly under cold water; drain well. In large saucepan, pour boiling water over rice; return to boil. Reduce heat and simmer gently for 45 minutes or until tender but not mushy; drain well. Transfer to lightly greased 13- × 9-inch (3.5 L) casserole.

■ In large skillet, melt butter over medium-high heat; sauté onion and mushrooms until tender, 5 to 8 minutes. Add to wild rice, mixing well.

■ Add turkey, stock, cream, chestnuts, pimiento, salt, and pepper to taste; mix well. Cover and bake in 350°F (180°C) oven for 40 minutes. Sprinkle cheese over casserole; bake, uncovered, for 15 to 20 minutes longer or until cheese is bubbling. Makes about 6 servings.

Knife-and-Fork Chicken and Avocado Sandwich

Long, slender rolls show off the layers of color in this delicious sandwich. Rubber gloves protect your hands from burning when you chop the chili pepper.

3 tbsp	lime juice	50 mL
1 tbsp	vegetable oil	15 mL
1/2 tsp	pepper	2 mL
1/4 tsp	dried oregano	1 mL
4	boneless skinless chicken breasts	4
1	avocado	1
2	tomatoes	2
2 tsp	finely chopped hot chili pepper	10 mL
1 tbsp	finely chopped red onion	15 mL
4	long braided poppy seed rolls or kaiser rolls	4
	Butter (optional)	
2 cups	shredded Monterey Jack or mild Cheddar cheese	500 mL

■ In bowl, stir together 2 tbsp (25 mL) of the lime juice, oil, pepper and oregano; add chicken, turning to coat well. Cover and marinate at room temperature for 30 minutes.

■ Remove chicken from marinade, reserving marinade. Broil chicken for 8 to 10 minutes or until no longer pink inside, turning once and brushing with reserved marinade. Transfer to plate; cover and keep warm.

■ Meanwhile, peel and halve avocado lengthwise; remove pit. In small bowl, mash half of the avocado. Dice 1 of the tomatoes; stir into avocado along with remaining lime juice, chili pepper and onion. Slice remaining avocado half and tomato.

■ Slice rolls lengthwise; broil, cut sides up, until lightly toasted. Butter rolls if desired.

■ Slice chicken into thin slices on diagonal. Spread 4 bottom halves of rolls with avocado mixture; top with chicken. Layer with avocado and tomato slices, pressing down lightly. Sprinkle with cheese. Broil for about 2 minutes or until cheese melts. Top with remaining rolls. Makes 4 servings.

Shrimp Rice Pilaf

Ham can be used instead of shrimp for a flavor variation. In fact, a combination of shrimp and ham is delicious. Serve with a vegetable salad and sorbet for dessert.

3 tbsp	unsalted butter	50 mL
2	cloves garlic, minced	2
1 lb	shrimp, peeled and deveined	500 g
1 cup	long-grain rice	250 mL
2 cups	chicken stock	500 mL
3 tbsp	chopped fresh dill	50 mL
	Salt and pepper	

■ In large saucepan, melt butter over medium heat; cook garlic until tender and fragrant but not browned, about 1 minute.

■ Add shrimp and mix well; stir in rice. Pour in stock and bring to boil; cover, reduce heat and simmer gently for 20 to 25 minutes or until liquid is absorbed. Stir in dill; season with salt and pepper to taste. Makes about 4 servings.

Sesame Fish with Zucchini and Tomatoes

Dinner will be ready in minutes when you serve this crunchy sautéed fish and zucchini with warm tomatoes. Accompany with a fresh cucumber salad. Buy fish fillets that are frozen in a solid block, not individually. Serve oatmeal cookies and melon wedges for a fine ending to the meal.

1 lb	frozen fish fillets	500 g
1	egg	1
2/3 cup	sesame seeds	150 mL
1/2 cup	fresh bread crumbs	125 mL
1 tbsp	finely chopped fresh dill (or 1 tsp/5 mL dillweed)	15 mL
1/2 tsp	salt	2 mL
4	small zucchini	4
1/4 cup	vegetable oil	50 mL
2	tomatoes, cut in wedges	2

■ Thaw fish at room temperature for 15 to 30 minutes or until easily cut with sharp knife. (Alternatively, microwave fish at Defrost or Medium-Low/30% for 4 minutes.)

■ In shallow dish, beat egg lightly. In sturdy plastic bag, combine sesame seeds, bread crumbs, dill and salt. Halve zucchini lengthwise.

■ With serrated knife, cut block of partially thawed fish crosswise into 4 pieces. Dip fish and zucchini into beaten egg; add to bag and shake to coat in sesame seed mixture.

■ In large skillet, heat oil over medium-high heat; cook fish for 7 minutes. Turn fish and add zucchini; cook for about 7 minutes longer or until zucchini is tender and fish flakes easily when tested with fork.

■ Transfer fish and zucchini to heated platter. Add tomato wedges to skillet; cook for about 1 minute or just until heated through. Arrange tomatoes attractively on platter. Makes about 4 servings.

Shrimp Rice Pilaf ▶

Shrimp and Mussel Stir-Fry

Garnish the platter with chopped green onion and lemon wedges for a spectacular presentation.

2 lb	mussels	1 kg
1 lb	small or medium shrimp	500 g
2 tbsp	vegetable oil	25 mL
2	cloves garlic, minced	2
1 tbsp	minced gingerroot	15 mL
1/4 tsp	hot pepper flakes	1 mL
2	carrots, diagonally sliced	2
1	onion, chopped	1
1	stalk celery, diagonally sliced	1
4	large mushrooms, sliced	4
1/2 cup	chicken stock or white wine	125 mL
1 tbsp	cornstarch	15 mL
1 tbsp	each soy sauce and oyster sauce	15 mL
2 cups	small broccoli florets	500 mL

■ Scrub mussels under cold water; remove any beards. Discard any that do not close. Peel and devein shrimp, leaving tails on. Set aside.

■ In wok or large skillet, heat oil over medium-high heat; stir-fry garlic, gingerroot and hot pepper flakes for 30 seconds. Add carrots, onion and celery; stir-fry for 2 minutes. Add mushrooms; stir-fry for 1 minute.

■ Add 1/4 cup (50 mL) of the stock and mussels; cook, stirring, for 4 to 5 minutes or until shells open. Discard any that do not open.

■ Combine remaining stock with cornstarch, soy sauce and oyster sauce; add to wok along with broccoli and shrimp. Cook for 2 to 3 minutes or until shrimp are pink, broccoli is tender-crisp and sauce is thickened. Makes 6 servings.

SUPER-EASY COMPANY MENU
Here's a simple menu for a dinner that's good enough for company. Serve Shrimp and Mussel Stir-Fry with steamed rice and a crisp tossed salad. Prepare an elegant fresh fruit and cheese platter for dessert.

Baked Salmon-Stuffed Potatoes

You can bake and stuff these potatoes a day in advance.

4	baking potatoes	4
1	can (7-1/2 oz/213 g) salmon, drained	1
1/2 cup	plain yogurt or sour cream	125 mL
1/4 cup	diced Cheddar cheese	50 mL
1 tbsp	chopped green onion	15 mL
1 tbsp	chopped fresh parsley or dill	15 mL
1 tbsp	lemon juice	15 mL
1/2 tsp	hot pepper sauce	2 mL
	Salt, pepper and paprika	
1/3 cup	shredded Cheddar cheese	75 mL

■ Scrub potatoes and prick with fork; bake in 400°F (200°C) oven for 45 to 55 minutes or until tender when gently squeezed.

■ In bowl, combine salmon, yogurt, diced cheese, onion, parsley, lemon juice and hot pepper sauce; season with salt, pepper and paprika to taste.

■ Cut 1/2-inch (1 cm) thick slice from top of each potato. Scoop out pulp, leaving 1/4-inch (5 mm) thick shell; stir pulp into salmon mixture, breaking up with fork.

■ Spoon filling into potato shells, mounding tops; sprinkle with shredded cheese. Bake in 400°F (200°C) oven for 15 to 20 minutes or until heated through and tops are crisp. Makes 4 servings.

Easy Oyster Stew

Called a "stew," this dish of lightly poached oysters is more like a soup. With already shucked oysters, this stew is quick to make, and both impressive and satisfying.

5 cups	milk	1.25 L
1/4 cup	fine soda-cracker crumbs	50 mL
1/4 cup	butter	50 mL
1-1/2 tsp	salt	7 mL
Pinch	each pepper and nutmeg	Pinch
2 cups	shucked oysters and their liquor	500 mL
2 tbsp	finely chopped fresh chives or parsley	25 mL

■ In saucepan, heat milk over low heat until bubbles form around edge. Add cracker crumbs, butter, salt, pepper and nutmeg.

■ Drain oysters, adding liquor to milk mixture; heat until butter has melted. Add oysters; simmer gently, uncovered, for about 3 minutes or just until oysters plump up and begin to curl around edges, being careful not to overcook.

■ Serve immediately; sprinkle with chives. Makes 6 servings.

Cioppino Pasta

Cioppino is a fish and seafood stew. In this version, it is adapted as a sauce for pasta. If you prefer to omit the shrimp and crab, you can substitute equal amounts of fish. This dish can be the star attraction of a buffet.

3 tbsp	olive oil	50 mL
1	onion, finely chopped	1
3	cloves garlic, finely chopped	3
1/4 tsp	hot pepper flakes	1 mL
1/4 tsp	dried oregano	1 mL
1/4 tsp	(approx) pepper	1 mL
2	cans (each 28 oz/796 mL) plum tomatoes, chopped (undrained)	2
1 cup	dry white wine	250 mL
1-1/2 lb	halibut steaks or fillets, cut in chunks	750 g
1 lb	shrimp, peeled and deveined	500 g
7 oz	frozen snow crab, thawed and cartilage removed	200 g
3 tbsp	chopped fresh parsley	50 mL
1 tsp	(approx) salt	5 mL
2 lb	rigatoni or penne	1 kg
1/2 cup	fresh bread crumbs (optional)	125 mL

■ In large skillet or Dutch oven, heat oil over medium heat; cook onion and garlic for 5 minutes or until tender and fragrant but not browned.

■ Stir in hot pepper flakes, oregano and pepper. Add tomatoes; cook, stirring to break up tomatoes, for 10 minutes or until most of the liquid has evaporated. Pour in wine; cook for 10 to 20 minutes or until reduced and thickened, stirring occasionally.

■ Add halibut, shrimp, crab, parsley and salt; cook, covered, for 5 to 10 minutes or just until fish and seafood are cooked through. *(Recipe can be prepared to this point, covered and refrigerated for up to 1 day; reheat before continuing.)*

■ Meanwhile, in large pot of boiling salted water, cook pasta until tender but firm; drain well and toss with seafood mixture. If too liquid, add bread crumbs and toss until crumbs absorb extra liquid. Taste and adjust seasoning with more salt and pepper if necessary. Makes about 8 servings.

Singapore Noodles with Pork and Peppers

This dish works well with whole grain pasta, but any other pasta can be substituted. It's also tasty made with chicken instead of pork. The cooked dish freezes well, too.

1 lb	pork loin	500 g
1 tbsp	vegetable oil	15 mL
1	leek (white and light green part only)	1
1	each sweet red, yellow and green pepper, seeded	1
2	large cloves garlic, minced	2
1-1/2 cups	chicken stock	375 mL
1/4 cup	oyster sauce	50 mL
1 tbsp	curry powder	15 mL
1 tbsp	cornstarch	15 mL
1 tbsp	cold water	15 mL
1/2 cup	chopped fresh parsley or coriander	125 mL
Dash	hot pepper sauce	Dash
3/4 lb	whole wheat spaghetti	375 g

■ Cut pork into 2- × 1/4-inch (5 cm × 5 mm) strips. In large skillet, heat oil over high heat; stir-fry pork for 3 to 4 minutes or until well browned. Remove and set aside.

■ Cut leek and sweet peppers into 1-1/2- × 1/4-inch (4 cm × 5 mm) strips. In same skillet, cover and cook leek, peppers, garlic and stock for 2 minutes; stir in oyster sauce and curry powder.

■ Blend cornstarch with water; stir into skillet along with pork. Bring to boil and cook, stirring, for 1 to 2 minutes or until heated through and thickened. Stir in parsley and hot pepper sauce.

■ Meanwhile, in large pot of boiling salted water, cook spaghetti for 8 to 10 minutes or until tender but firm. Drain well. In large bowl, toss spaghetti with meat mixture. Makes 6 servings.

Classic Lasagna

Fresh thin pasta from pasta shops is best to use for this multilayered lasagna, but dry noodles work wonderfully well, too.

3/4 lb	lasagna noodles	375 g
1 cup	freshly grated Parmesan cheese	250 mL
2 tbsp	butter	25 mL

MEAT SAUCE		
2 tbsp	olive oil	25 mL
1	onion, chopped	1
2	cloves garlic, minced	2
1	carrot, chopped	1
1	stalk celery, chopped	1
1/2 lb	lean ground beef	250 g
1/2 lb	lean ground pork	250 g
1/2 cup	dry white wine or chicken stock	125 mL
1	can (28 oz/796 mL) plum tomatoes, puréed	1
1 tsp	salt	5 mL
1/2 tsp	pepper	2 mL
1/2 cup	whipping cream	125 mL

BESCIAMELLA SAUCE		
1/4 cup	butter	50 mL
1/4 cup	all-purpose flour	50 mL
3 cups	milk	750 mL
1 tsp	salt	5 mL
1/2 tsp	pepper	2 mL
1/4 tsp	nutmeg	1 mL

■ **Meat Sauce:** In Dutch oven, heat oil over medium heat; cook onion, garlic, carrot and celery for about 8 minutes or until fragrant.

■ Add beef and pork, breaking up with spoon. Pour in wine; cook for about 5 minutes or until almost evaporated. Add tomatoes, salt and pepper; bring to boil. Reduce heat to medium-low; simmer gently for 20 minutes. Add cream; cook for 20 to 25 minutes or until thickened. Let cool for 30 minutes.

■ **Besciamella Sauce:** In saucepan, melt butter over medium heat; whisk in flour and cook, stirring, for 2 minutes without browning. Whisk in milk and bring to boil; reduce heat to medium-low and cook, stirring, for 10 minutes or until thickened. Stir in salt, pepper and nutmeg. Let cool for 30 minutes.

■ In large pot of boiling salted water, cook noodles until almost tender, 2 minutes for fresh, 6 to 8 minutes for dried. Drain and rinse under cold water; drain and pat dry. Arrange one-fifth of the noodles in single layer in greased 13- × 9-inch (3 L) baking dish. Cover with one-third of the Meat Sauce, one-fifth of the noodles, one-third of the Besciamella Sauce and one-third of the Parmesan. Repeat layers; top with remaining noodles, Meat Sauce, Besciamella Sauce and Parmesan. Dot with butter. Bake in 375°F (190°C) oven for 40 to 45 minutes or until bubbling. Let stand for 10 minutes. Makes 8 servings.

Manicotti with Sausages and Red Pepper Sauce

The sausage filling gives zip to this pleasantly spiced version of manicotti. Use sweet or spicy sausages.

3 tbsp	olive or vegetable oil	50 mL
1	onion, finely chopped	1
2	cloves garlic, minced	2
1/4 tsp	hot pepper flakes	1 mL
1-1/2 lb	Italian sausage, casings removed	750 g
1	pkg (10 oz/284 g) spinach, cooked, squeezed dry and chopped	1
1 tsp	salt	5 mL
1/2 tsp	pepper	2 mL
1	egg, lightly beaten	1
1/2 cup	whipping cream	125 mL
1 cup	freshly grated Parmesan cheese	250 mL
3 tbsp	chopped fresh basil (optional)	50 mL
2 tbsp	chopped fresh parsley	25 mL
1 lb	cooked manicotti noodles	500 g
	Red Pepper Sauce (recipe follows)	
1 cup	shredded Swiss or mozzarella cheese	250 mL

■ In skillet, heat oil over medium-high heat; sauté onion, garlic and hot pepper flakes for about 3 minutes or until softened. Crumble in meat; cook until browned.

■ Add spinach, salt and pepper; let cool slightly. Stir in egg, cream and half of the Parmesan. Add basil (if using) and parsley. Taste and adjust seasoning if necessary. Using 24 unbroken cooked noodles, spoon about 3 tbsp (50 mL) meat mixture into each.

■ Spread 1 cup (250 mL) of the Red Pepper Sauce into each of two 13- × 9-inch (3.5 L) baking dishes. Arrange filled manicotti in one layer over sauce. Cover with remaining sauce.

■ Sprinkle with remaining Parmesan and Swiss cheese. Bake in 350°F (180°C) oven for 30 to 35 minutes or until top is browned and bubbling. Makes 10 to 12 servings.

RED PEPPER SAUCE

3	sweet red peppers	3
3 tbsp	olive oil	50 mL
1	onion, chopped	1
2	cloves garlic, finely chopped	2
1	can (28 oz/796 mL) plum tomatoes (undrained)	1
1/4 tsp	hot pepper sauce	1 mL
	Salt and pepper	
1/2 cup	whipping cream	125 mL

■ Using vegetable peeler, peel red peppers; chop coarsely. In large saucepan, heat oil over medium heat; cook onion and garlic for about 5 minutes or until tender and fragrant. Add red peppers; cook for 5 minutes or until peppers start to wilt.

■ Add tomatoes, breaking up with spoon; bring to boil. Reduce heat and simmer, covered, for 30 minutes. Purée mixture in blender or food processor. Add hot pepper sauce, and salt and pepper to taste. Stir in cream and heat through. Makes about 5 cups (1.25 L).

Baked Tortellini with Three Cheeses

This easy casserole filled with creamy cheese and colorful green peas is a great make-ahead dish for a hassle-free supper hour.

1	pkg (350 g) meat- or cheese-filled tortellini	1
3 tbsp	butter	50 mL
1 cup	fresh bread crumbs	250 mL
2	cloves garlic, minced	2
1	small onion, chopped	1
4 tsp	all-purpose flour	20 mL
1 cup	milk	250 mL
1 tsp	dried basil	5 mL
	Salt and pepper	
1 cup	shredded low-fat mozzarella cheese	250 mL
1 cup	low-fat cottage cheese	250 mL
1/2 cup	freshly grated Parmesan cheese	125 mL
1-1/2 cups	frozen peas	375 mL

■ In large pot of boiling salted water, cook tortellini according to package directions. Drain well and transfer to greased 8-cup (2 L) shallow casserole.

■ Meanwhile, in large skillet, melt butter. Transfer 1 tbsp (15 mL) to small bowl and stir in bread crumbs; set aside.

■ Add garlic and onion to skillet; cook over medium heat, stirring often, for 4 minutes or until onion is softened. Sprinkle with flour and cook, stirring, for 1 minute. Gradually stir in milk; sprinkle with three-quarters of the basil, and salt and pepper to taste. Cook, stirring, for 2 to 3 minutes or until thickened and bubbly.

■ Remove from heat and stir in mozzarella, cottage cheese and Parmesan until smooth; pour over tortellini in casserole. Rinse peas under hot water; gently stir into casserole.

■ Stir remaining basil into reserved bread crumb mixture; sprinkle over casserole. *(Recipe can be prepared to this point, covered and refrigerated for up to 6 hours.)* Bake, uncovered, in 375°F (190°C) oven for 20 to 30 minutes or until bubbling. Makes 4 servings.

Layered Macaroni and Cheese Casserole

Layers of ham and spinach provide color to macaroni and cheese. A celery, carrot and cabbage coleslaw adds pleasing texture contrast.

1	pkg (10 oz/284 g) spinach, trimmed	1
3 cups	elbow macaroni	750 mL
1/4 cup	butter	50 mL
1/4 cup	all-purpose flour	50 mL
3-1/2 cups	milk	875 mL
1/4 tsp	(approx) white pepper	1 mL
Pinch	each cayenne pepper and nutmeg	Pinch
4 cups	shredded old Cheddar cheese (about 1 lb/500 g)	1 L
1-1/2 cups	fresh bread crumbs	375 mL
6 oz	thinly sliced cooked ham	175 g

■ Rinse spinach; shake off excess water. In saucepan with just the water clinging to leaves, cook spinach just until wilted; drain and let cool. Squeeze dry and chop coarsely; place in bowl and set aside.

■ In large saucepan of lightly salted boiling water, cook macaroni until tender but firm, about 7 minutes. Drain well and return to saucepan.

■ Meanwhile, in another saucepan, melt 3 tbsp (45 mL) of the butter over medium heat; blend in flour and cook, stirring, for 1 minute. Stir in milk, white and cayenne peppers and nutmeg; cook, stirring, until thickened and smooth, about 5 minutes. Mix in 3 cups (750 mL) of the cheese until melted. Reserve 1/2 cup (125 mL) of the sauce. Stir remaining sauce into macaroni; set aside.

■ To spinach in bowl, add reserved sauce, 1/2 cup (125 mL) of the bread crumbs and 1/2 cup (125 mL) of the remaining cheese; season lightly with white pepper and set aside.

■ Spoon one-third of the macaroni mixture into well-greased 12-cup (3 L) deep casserole dish. Layer ham on top. Spread with another third of the macaroni mixture. Spread spinach mixture over top. Cover with remaining macaroni mixture.

■ Combine remaining bread crumbs, cheese and butter; sprinkle evenly over casserole. *(Recipe can be prepared to this point, covered and refrigerated for up to 24 hours.)* Bake in 350°F (180°C) oven for 40 to 50 minutes or until topping is crisp and golden brown. Makes about 6 servings.

Light Lasagna

Ground chicken instead of beef, low-fat cottage cheese and skim mozzarella all make this lasagna lighter than most.

1 tbsp	olive oil	15 mL
1	onion, chopped	1
3	green onions, chopped	3
2	cloves garlic, minced	2
1/4 tsp	hot pepper flakes	1 mL
1 lb	ground chicken	500 g
1 cup	finely chopped carrots	250 mL
1 cup	finely chopped celery	250 mL
1-1/2 cups	finely chopped sweet red pepper	375 mL
2	cans (each 28 oz/796 mL) plum tomatoes, puréed	2
1 tsp	(approx) salt	5 mL
1/2 tsp	(approx) pepper	2 mL
1/4 cup	chopped fresh parsley	50 mL
3/4 lb	lasagna noodles	375 g
2 cups	low-fat cottage cheese	500 mL
2 cups	shredded skim mozzarella cheese (about 1/2 lb/250 g)	500 mL

■ In Dutch oven, heat oil over medium heat; cook onion, green onions, garlic and hot pepper flakes for about 5 minutes or until fragrant.

■ Add chicken and cook, stirring, for 5 minutes or until no longer pink. Add carrots, celery and sweet pepper; cook, stirring, for 5 minutes. Add tomatoes and bring to boil. Add 1 tsp (5 mL) salt and 1/2 tsp (2 mL) pepper. Reduce heat to medium-low and simmer gently for 35 to 45 minutes or until thickened. Stir in parsley.

■ In large pot of boiling salted water, cook noodles until almost tender, 2 minutes for fresh, 6 to 8 minutes for dried. Drain and rinse under cold water; drain and pat dry.

■ Season cottage cheese with salt and pepper to taste. Arrange one-quarter of the noodles in single layer in greased 13- × 9-inch (3 L) baking dish. Spread with half of the cottage cheese, then one-quarter of the sauce; sprinkle with one-quarter of the mozzarella. Repeat layer of noodles, sauce and mozzarella. Repeat layer of noodles, cottage cheese, sauce and mozzarella; top with layer of noodles, sauce and mozzarella.

■ Cover with foil and bake in 375°F (190°C) oven for 50 minutes; uncover and bake for 10 minutes longer or until bubbling. Let stand for 10 minutes. Makes 8 servings.

Pasta with Shrimp Sauce

This dish is a dieter's dream — rich in flavor and low in calories.

1 cup	canned tomatoes (undrained)	250 mL
1/4 cup	dry white wine	50 mL
1	small onion, sliced	1
1/2 tsp	dried basil	2 mL
Pinch	each salt and pepper	Pinch
1/4 lb	shrimp, peeled and deveined	125 g
1	small zucchini, shredded	1
1	clove garlic, minced	1
1 tbsp	chopped fresh parsley	15 mL
1-1/2 tsp	olive oil	7 mL
6 oz	spaghetti, fettuccine or linguine	175 g

■ In saucepan, combine tomatoes, wine, onion, basil, salt and pepper; bring to boil. Reduce heat to medium-low; cook, uncovered, for 20 minutes, stirring frequently.

■ Add shrimp, zucchini, garlic, parsley and oil; simmer for 5 minutes or just until shrimp are pink but not overcooked.

■ Meanwhile, in large saucepan of boiling salted water, cook pasta until tender but firm; drain well. Arrange on serving plates; top with shrimp sauce. Makes 2 servings.

PREPARING PERFECT PASTA
Cook pasta in a large pot that allows plenty of room for the water to boil briskly and pasta to cook without being crowded.

• Bring water to a rolling boil; add salt, then add the pasta all at once. Bring back to boil. Stir to separate pasta and boil quickly.

• Cooking times vary depending on size and shape of pasta and whether it is fresh or dried. Fresh pasta cooks in about 2 minutes after the water returns to a boil, dried pasta in 5 to 10 minutes.

• Cook only until al dente (tender but firm). Drain cooked pasta in a colander and use immediately.

Cheesy Baked Spaghetti

Everyone loves spaghetti, and this baked version is a favorite with cooks, too, because it can be prepared ahead. It's delicious made with either sweet or hot Italian sausage.

2 tbsp	(approx) vegetable oil	25 mL
4	cloves garlic, minced	4
1	large onion, chopped	1
1	sweet green pepper, cubed	1
2 cups	sliced mushrooms	500 mL
2 lb	Italian sausage	1 kg
1	can (28 oz/796 mL) tomatoes (undrained)	1
2 tsp	dried oregano	10 mL
1 tsp	dried thyme	5 mL
1/2 tsp	fennel seeds	2 mL
1/4 tsp	pepper	1 mL
Pinch	hot pepper flakes	Pinch
6 oz	spaghetti	175 g
1/4 cup	chopped fresh parsley	50 mL
	TOPPING	
1/4 cup	butter	50 mL
1/4 cup	all-purpose flour	50 mL
2 cups	milk	500 mL
2	eggs, beaten	2
1 tsp	dry mustard	5 mL
2 cups	shredded mozzarella cheese	500 mL
1/2 cup	freshly grated Parmesan cheese	125 mL
2 tbsp	fine dry bread crumbs	25 mL

■ In large heavy nonstick saucepan, heat oil over medium heat; cook garlic, onion, green pepper and mushrooms until softened, about 7 minutes. Using slotted spoon, transfer to bowl.

■ Cut sausage into 1/2-inch (1 cm) thick slices. Add more oil to pan if needed; increase heat to high and brown sausage in 2 batches. Drain off fat; return onion mixture to pan. Add tomatoes, oregano, thyme, fennel seeds, pepper and hot pepper flakes; bring to boil. Reduce heat, cover and simmer, stirring often, for 30 minutes.

■ Meanwhile, break spaghetti into 3-inch (8 cm) lengths. In large pot of boiling salted water, cook spaghetti until tender but firm, about 8 minutes. Drain well; add to tomato mixture. Add parsley. Taste and adjust seasoning. Transfer to 16-cup (4 L) baking dish or two 8-inch (2 L) square baking pans. Set aside.

■ **Topping:** In heavy saucepan, melt butter over medium heat; stir in flour and cook for 1 minute, stirring constantly. Gradually stir in milk. Bring to boil; cook, stirring constantly, until thickened and smooth, about 5 minutes. Let cool slightly; stir in eggs, mustard and mozzarella cheese until cheese has melted. Spoon evenly over spaghetti mixture.

■ Stir together Parmesan and bread crumbs; sprinkle evenly over egg mixture. *(Casserole can be prepared to this point, covered and refrigerated for up to 8 hours. Let stand at room temperature for 20 minutes before baking.)* Bake in 375°F (190°C) oven for 35 to 40 minutes or until top is crusty and golden. Let stand for 10 minutes. Makes about 8 servings.

Vegetable Chili with Cheddar

Serve this spicy vegetable chili with hot corn bread and a crunchy cabbage and carrot slaw.

1	eggplant (about 1 lb/500 g)	1
2 tsp	salt	10 mL
1/4 cup	olive oil	50 mL
3 cups	diced sweet red and green peppers	750 mL
2 cups	coarsely chopped onions	500 mL
4	cloves garlic, minced	4
2 tbsp	chili powder	25 mL
1 tbsp	each cumin, dried basil and oregano	15 mL
1-1/2 tsp	pepper	7 mL
2	cans (each 28 oz/796 mL) plum tomatoes	2
1	can (19 oz/540 mL) red kidney beans, drained	1
1	can (19 oz/540 mL) chick-peas, drained	1
4 cups	shredded old Cheddar cheese (about 1 lb/500 g)	1 L

■ Chop eggplant into 1/2-inch (1 cm) cubes. Place in colander and sprinkle with salt; let stand for 1 hour to drain. Rinse and pat dry.

■ In large heavy saucepan, heat oil over medium heat; cook eggplant, red and green peppers, onions and garlic for about 6 minutes or until softened.

■ Add chili powder, cumin, basil, oregano and pepper; cook for 3 minutes, stirring. Add tomatoes, breaking up with fork, and bring to boil; reduce heat and simmer, stirring frequently, for about 30 minutes or until vegetables are tender.

■ Add kidney beans and chick-peas; cook for about 15 minutes or until chili has thickened. Taste and adjust seasoning. *(Recipe can be prepared to this point, cooled, covered and frozen for up to 3 months or refrigerated for up to 2 days. Heat through before continuing.)*

■ Transfer chili to shallow 10-cup (2.5 L) baking dish; sprinkle with Cheddar. Broil for 4 minutes or until cheese melts and has browned. Makes about 6 servings.

Microwave Spaghetti Squash with Cheese Sauce

Spaghetti squash makes a light alternative to pasta. Accompany the dish with seed bread and a green salad tossed with a lemon vinaigrette.

1	spaghetti squash (about 3-1/2 lb/1.75 kg)	1
	SAUCE	
1/4 cup	butter	50 mL
1/2 cup	cream cheese, cubed	125 mL
2 tbsp	light cream	25 mL
2 tbsp	freshly grated Parmesan cheese	25 mL
	Salt and pepper	
2 tbsp	each chopped green onion and toasted walnuts	25 mL

■ Pierce squash in 4 places; place in large microwaveable dish. Microwave at High for 4 minutes; turn over and cook for 4 minutes. Let stand for 10 minutes.

■ Halve squash lengthwise, remove seeds; cover and cook each half for about 4 minutes or until fork can ease out strands of squash. With fork, pull out strands and return to shells; cover and set aside.

■ **Sauce:** In 8-cup (2 L) microwaveable measure or casserole, microwave butter at High for 25 seconds. Add cream cheese; microwave at High for 1-1/2 minutes or until cheese has softened, stirring frequently. Whisk in cream and Parmesan. Season with salt and pepper to taste.

■ Stir squash into cheese sauce; mix together until well coated. Sprinkle each serving with green onion and walnuts. Makes about 4 servings.

SAY CHEESE!

Just stop your cart at the supermarket dairy case and feast on the variety of cheese — creamy whole-milk mozzarella, well-ripened Camembert, sweet and nutty ivory-colored Emmenthal. Keep your eyes open for a wedge of Brie and red doorstop spheres of Gouda cheese. There's bound to be a selection of Cheddar — mild, medium, old and extra-old — in orange and white slabs, along with its cousin, buttery Colby.

• As our interest in lighter, vegetable-based dishes has increased, so has the imaginative use of cheese as the star of the meal. In this section, we've included cheesy one-dish meals that are perfect for your family suppers and casual entertaining menus.

Baked Rice with Red Pepper, Corn and Colby Cheese

Brick, Fontina, Friulano, Monterey Jack, Gouda and Swiss cheese can all be substituted for the Colby in this hearty vegetarian dish.

3 cups	water	750 mL
1-1/2 cups	parboiled long-grain rice	375 mL
1/2 tsp	salt	2 mL
2 tbsp	butter	25 mL
1	large sweet red pepper, cored and seeded	1
2 cups	shredded Colby cheese (about 1/2 lb/250 g)	500 mL
1/2 cup	cooked corn kernels	125 mL
1/2 cup	sliced green onions	125 mL
1/4 tsp	hot pepper sauce	1 mL
1 cup	sour cream	250 mL
2/3 cup	freshly grated Parmesan cheese	150 mL
1/4 cup	coarse dry bread crumbs	50 mL

■ In heavy saucepan, bring water to boil. Add rice and salt; reduce heat to low, cover and cook for about 25 minutes or until rice is tender and liquid absorbed. Stir in butter; set aside.

■ Meanwhile, in small saucepan of boiling water, cook red pepper for 3 minutes or until skin has loosened; let cool slightly. Peel and chop coarsely.

■ Add red pepper, Colby, corn, green onions and hot pepper sauce to rice; mix together. Transfer to shallow greased 8-cup (2 L) baking dish, pressing down gently. *(Recipe can be prepared to this point, covered and refrigerated for up to 1 day.)*

■ Spread sour cream over rice mixture; sprinkle with Parmesan and bread crumbs. Bake in 400°F (200°C) oven for 20 to 30 minutes or until heated through and topping is browned. Makes about 6 servings.

Tamale Pie

Traditional tamales are little stuffed dumplings wrapped in corn husks; they require considerable practice to prepare quickly. This version eliminates the husks and the dumplings by layering the cornmeal, bean and tomato mixtures in a baking dish to make a chill-chasing main course.

1/2 cup	butter, softened	125 mL
1-1/2 cups	cornmeal	375 mL
1 cup	all-purpose flour	250 mL
1 tsp	cumin	5 mL
1/4 tsp	salt	1 mL
2-1/2 cups	warm water	625 mL

	FILLING	
1	can (14 oz/398 mL) kidney beans, drained	1
2	cloves garlic, minced	2
1/4 tsp	salt	1 mL
1	can (14 oz/398 mL) tomato sauce	1
1 tsp	dried oregano	5 mL
1/2 tsp	allspice	2 mL
1	hot chili pepper, seeded and minced	1
1	sweet green pepper, diced	1
1	onion, chopped	1
	Celery leaves (optional)	

■ In bowl, beat butter until creamy; beat in cornmeal, flour, cumin and salt until blended. Gradually beat in water; set aside.

■ **Filling:** In bowl, combine beans, garlic, salt, tomato sauce, oregano, allspice, hot chili pepper, green pepper and onion.

■ Spread half of the cornmeal batter in greased 8-cup (2 L) shallow casserole. Spread with bean mixture; spread remaining batter over top.

■ Bake in 325°F (160°C) oven for about 1 hour or until batter has set. Garnish with celery leaves (if using). Makes 8 servings.

Raclette Casserole

A Swiss dish, raclette is simply cheese melted by the fire, then usually scraped onto potatoes. This is a delicious casserole version. Swiss-type cheeses, such as Emmenthal, can be substituted for Oka cheese. Round out the meal with a tossed green salad, pickled gherkins and pearl onions.

6	**large new potatoes (about 2-1/2 lb/1.25 kg)**	6
1	**large carrot**	1
1	**large stalk broccoli**	1
2 tbsp	**butter**	25 mL
3 cups	**sliced mushrooms (about 1/2 lb/250 g)**	750 mL
	Salt and pepper	
6 cups	**shredded Oka cheese (about 1-1/2 lb/750 g)**	1.5 L

■ Peel potatoes if desired. In large saucepan of boiling salted water, cook potatoes for 20 to 30 minutes or just until tender.

■ Meanwhile, diagonally slice carrot into 1/4-inch (5 mm) thick slices; add to saucepan during last 5 minutes of cooking time. With slotted spoon, remove potatoes and carrot; let cool slightly. Slice potatoes thinly; set aside. Set carrots aside separately.

■ Peel broccoli stalk; cut stalk and florets into bite-size pieces. Add to saucepan of boiling water; cook for 2 minutes. Drain and refresh under cold water; set aside. In skillet, melt butter over medium heat; cook mushrooms, stirring occasionally, for about 6 minutes or just until tender.

■ In shallow greased 8-cup (2 L) baking dish, arrange half of the potatoes in overlapping slices. Season with salt and pepper to taste. Sprinkle 2 cups (500 mL) of the cheese over potatoes. Layer carrot, broccoli and mushrooms over cheese. Season with salt and pepper to taste.

■ Sprinkle 1 cup (250 mL) of the cheese over vegetables. Top with overlapping slices of remaining potatoes. Season with salt and pepper to taste. Sprinkle with remaining cheese. *(Recipe can be prepared to this point, covered and refrigerated for up to 2 hours.)*

■ Bake in 350°F (180°C) oven for 30 to 40 minutes or until heated through and cheese has melted. Broil for 1 to 2 minutes or until top is browned. Makes about 6 servings.

Cheddar-Corn Impossible Pie

The flour mixture in this quick, easy supper dish magically forms a very thin, tender base for the zesty custard filling. Serve with chili sauce and a salad of romaine lettuce and thin onion slices. Just omit the bacon for a vegetarian dish.

2 tbsp	dry bread crumbs	25 mL
10	slices bacon, cooked and crumbled (optional)	10
1 cup	shredded mild Cheddar cheese	250 mL
1	onion, minced	1
Half	sweet green pepper, diced	Half
1 cup	canned or thawed corn niblets	250 mL
Pinch	salt	Pinch
1/4 tsp	black pepper	1 mL
Pinch	cayenne pepper	Pinch
1/2 cup	all-purpose flour	125 mL
1 tsp	baking powder	5 mL
2 tbsp	shortening	25 mL
4	eggs	4
2 cups	milk	500 mL

■ Butter 10-inch (25 cm) quiche pan or pie plate; sprinkle with bread crumbs.

■ In bowl, combine bacon (if using), cheese, onion, green pepper, corn, salt, black pepper and cayenne pepper; sprinkle over bread crumbs.

■ In small bowl, stir together flour and baking powder; cut in shortening until in fine crumbs.

■ In separate bowl and using mixer or in food processor, blend together eggs, flour mixture and milk until smooth; pour over bacon mixture. Bake in 350°F (180°C) oven for 45 to 50 minutes or until knife inserted in centre comes out clean. Let stand for 5 minutes. Makes 4 servings.

Spaghetti Frittata

This Italian-style omelette makes a quick, low-cost dinner. You can serve it with your favorite tomato sauce or chili sauce if you like.

1/2 lb	spaghetti	250 g
1/3 cup	freshly grated Parmesan cheese	75 mL
1/4 cup	butter	50 mL
2 tbsp	chopped fresh parsley	25 mL
4	eggs	4
1/2 tsp	each salt and pepper	2 mL

■ In saucepan of boiling salted water, cook spaghetti until tender but firm. Drain well and return to pan. Stir in cheese, 3 tbsp (50 mL) of the butter and parsley; let cool slightly.

■ In small bowl, beat eggs, salt and pepper; add to spaghetti mixture, mixing well.

■ In large nonstick skillet, heat remaining butter over medium heat until foaming; pour in spaghetti mixture and spread evenly. Cook for 4 to 5 minutes or until bottom is golden brown. Loosen with spatula; invert onto plate. Slide frittata back into skillet and cook for 3 to 4 minutes or until bottom is golden brown. Cut into wedges to serve. Makes 4 servings.

STORING EGGS

Eggs are perishable. Store them in your refrigerator, large ends up, in the container in which you bought them rather than on the refrigerator door where vibrations and temperature changes can affect them. Store eggs away from strong-smelling foods because they can absorb odors.

Cheddar Cheese and Spinach Enchiladas

Enchiladas are soft tortillas rolled around vegetable, cheese or meat fillings and topped with tomato, green chili or cheese sauce. Use the soft type of tortilla, not the crisp taco-type. Look for them in bags in the frozen or refrigerated section of the supermarket or in cans in the Mexican food section.

3 tbsp	vegetable oil	50 mL
1	large onion, chopped	1
2	cloves garlic, minced	2
2	pkg (each 10 oz/284 g) spinach, chopped	2
1/2 cup	sour cream	125 mL
	Salt and pepper	
16	fresh or canned 16-inch (15 cm) tortillas	16
2-1/2 cups	shredded Cheddar cheese	625 mL
	SAUCE	
2 tbsp	butter	25 mL
2 tbsp	all-purpose flour	25 mL
1 cup	hot milk	250 mL
1-1/2 cups	shredded Cheddar cheese	375 mL
1 cup	sour cream	250 mL
1 tbsp	chopped fresh or canned jalapeño or green chili pepper*	15 mL
	Pepper	

■ In large saucepan, heat half of the oil over medium heat; cook onion until tender, 3 to 5 minutes. Stir in garlic. Add spinach; cook, stirring, for about 3 minutes or until spinach has wilted and liquid has evaporated. Remove from heat; stir in sour cream. Season with salt and pepper to taste.

■ In skillet, heat remaining oil over medium heat; heat 1 tortilla, turning once, for 30 seconds or until softened. Transfer to paper towel.

■ Spread heaping tablespoonful (15 mL) spinach mixture down centre of tortilla. Sprinkle with some of the cheese and roll up. Place seam side down in 2 greased 13- × 9-inch (3.5 L) baking dishes. Repeat with remaining tortillas.

■ **Sauce:** In saucepan, melt butter over low heat; stir in flour and cook, stirring, for 1 minute. Add hot milk and increase heat to medium-high; cook, stirring with whisk, until boiling and thickened. Reduce heat to low and simmer for 2 minutes.

■ Stir in Cheddar cheese, sour cream, jalapeño, and pepper to taste until cheese has melted. Pour over enchiladas. *(Recipe can be prepared to this point, cooled, covered and refrigerated for up to 2 days.)*

■ Bake, uncovered, in 350°F (180°C) oven for 25 to 30 minutes or until heated through. Makes 6 to 8 servings.

*Green chilies are milder than jalapeño peppers; add more to taste.

Credits

Recipes in THE CANADIAN LIVING COOKING COLLECTION have been created by the *Canadian Living* Test Kitchen and by the following food writers from across Canada: **Elizabeth Baird, Karen Brown, Joanna Burkhard, James Chatto, Diane Clement, David Cohlmeyer, Pam Collacott, Bonnie Baker Cowan, Pierre Dubrulle, Eileen Dwillies, Nancy Enright, Carol Ferguson, Margaret Fraser, Susan Furlan, Anita Goldberg, Barb Holland, Patricia Jamieson, Arlene Lappin, Anne Lindsay, Lispeth Lodge, Mary McGrath, Susan Mendelson, Bernard Meyer, Beth Moffatt, Rose Murray, Iris Raven, Gerry Shikatani, Jill Snider, Kay Spicer, Linda Stephen, Bonnie Stern, Lucy Waverman, Carol White, Ted Whittaker and Cynny Willet.**

The full-color photographs throughout are by Canada's leading food photographers, including **Fred Bird, Doug Bradshaw, Christopher Campbell, Nino D'Angelo, Frank Grant, Michael Kohn, Suzanne McCormick, Claude Noel, John Stephens** and **Mike Visser.**

Editorial and Production Staff: Hugh Brewster, Susan Barrable, Catherine Fraccaro, Wanda Nowakowska, Sandra L. Hall, Beverley Renahan and Bernice Eisenstein.

Index

LOOK FOR THESE BESTSELLING COOKBOOKS FROM *CANADIAN LIVING*

The most trusted name in Canadian cooking

New this Fall!
CANADIAN LIVING'S COUNTRY COOKING
Rediscover the familiar tastes of country cooking at its comforting best in the pages of this beautiful full-color cookbook. Each of the more than 200 dishes featured here is brimming over with flavor and honest, great taste....*$27.00 hardcover*

THE CANADIAN LIVING COOKBOOK
Beautiful yet practical, this Canadian classic features over 525 recipes by Canada's finest food writers and a host of cooking hints, charts and ideas....*$35.00 hardcover*

THE CANADIAN LIVING LIGHT & HEALTHY COOKBOOK
Over 150 nutritious *and* delicious recipes make it easy to prepare healthy, balanced meals for the whole family. Includes handy nutrition charts for each recipe plus health and food facts....*$20.00 softcover*

THE CANADIAN LIVING MICROWAVE COOKBOOK
Over 175 delicious recipes — plus microwaving basics, charts and tips — make this an invaluable book no microwave owner should be without....*$27.00 hardcover*

THE CANADIAN LIVING RUSH-HOUR COOKBOOK
This easy-to-use cookbook features over 200 recipes and 100 menus for fast and tasty everyday meals that can be prepared in under 60 minutes. A must for today's busy cooks....*$27.00 hardcover*

THE CANADIAN LIVING BARBECUE COOKBOOK
Over 175 tested recipes for easy and delicious summer cooking plus the latest information on barbecue equipment and techniques....*$19.95 softcover*

THE CANADIAN LIVING ENTERTAINING COOKBOOK
A gorgeous gift book featuring over 350 easy-to-prepare recipes for every entertaining occasion. It includes inventive menus plus the latest ideas for setting the table — and the mood!...*$34.95 hardcover*

Also from Canadian Living
GLORIOUS CHRISTMAS CRAFTS
Over 135 imaginative ways to make Christmas extra special....*$24.95 hardcover*